EXPERIENCES AND PLACES

By the same author

FIRST DAY

STRAIGHT OR CURLY?

POEMS, 1935–48

EXPERIENCES
AND
PLACES

New Poems by

CLIFFORD DYMENT

LONDON
J. M. DENT & SONS LTD

by
J. M. DENT & SONS LTD
Aldine House · Bedford Street · London
Made in Great Britain
at
The Aldine Press · Letchworth · Herts
First published 1955

TO

BARNETT FREEDMAN

affectionately

CONTENTS

FOREWORD

Like many poets, I suppose, I have often been asked if I have ever dreamed a poem. Until recently my answer has been no. During the last year or so, however, stories and fragments of verse have sometimes occurred to me in dream. On one occasion I dreamed a poem intermittently over a period of about a week, parts of it being visible to me as dark handwriting on a greyish substance and parts appearing as landscape. In these dreams I was aware of being within the poem, of the poem experiencing me rather than I the poem. On waking—immediately, before the vividness of the dream faded, which of course it did quickly—I transcribed the fragments which had appeared to me as writing; and words describing the scenes of which I had been a part came without any conscious effort at composition. The resulting poem I include here as the last in the book, because I think it has a 'sense' that makes it interesting in view of the way in which it came into existence.

There are two other poems in this collection about which I should like to say a few words—*The King of the Wood* and *The Children*. These are related in that when writing them I had in mind the mythological figure of the King of the Wood at Nemi, who was 'a priest and a murderer.' The idea in the two poems is that the 'priest and the murderer' is life itself, the law of nature being that life must slay life for life's sake.

Some of the poems have previously been printed in magazines and anthologies and I wish to thank the editors of these publications for permission to include such poems here: the *Listener*, *London Magazine*, *New Statesman and Nation*, *Poetry and Poverty*, *Poetry Review*, *Gala Day London* (Harvill Press), *New Poems 1952* and *1955* (P.E.N. Club and Michael Joseph).

C. D.

THE KING OF THE WOOD

Winter: winter in the woods
Is the bone that was the beauty,
The bough that lives the leaf:
The food supplies sink low
And the hedgehog and badger know the hour is late.

Comes snow—the scouting flakes
Nipping out of the north
Followed by bulky brigades
Falling with formidable lust
On land where evil and warm the weevil sleeps.

Spring: the leaves of the chestnut
Hang in the branches like bats;
Bluebells flood into valleys
Where butterflies dry wet wings
And the cock bird lords it in song on his terrain.

This is the season of primrose,
Woodruff, and anemone—
And the season of caterpillars
Of the mottled umber moth
Fattening ambition in a thousand worlds of plenty.

Summer: welcome the woods
When the air sweats in the sun!
Here is a draught of shade
In a cellar deep and dark
Where barrels are so tall they sway like trees.

Now ants are on the hunt
Each for a swag of syrup—
And the felted beech coccus
Seeks out the straight young tree
To lay the foundation stone of a leaning tower.

Autumn: the sky more blue
Than any flower or crystal;
The yellow and wrinkled face
Of the wood is streaked with wounds
As the catkins of the birches slide to the soil.

Burgled boxes with ermine
Lining drop their conkers
Among loot of acorns for squirrels—
And into the earth descends
The cockchafer beetle's larva to mine a future.

THE CARPENTER

With a jack plane in his hands
My father the carpenter
Massaged the wafering wood,
Making it white and true.

He was skilful with his saws,
Handsaw, bowsaw, hacksaw,
And ripsaw with fishes' teeth
That chewed a plank in a second.

He was fond of silver bits,
The twist and countersink—
And the auger in its pit
Chucking shavings over its shoulder.

I remember my father's hands,
For they were supple and strong
With fingers that were lovers—
Sensuous strokers of wood:

He fondled the oak, the strong-man
Who holds above his head
A record-breaking lift
Of thick commingled boughs;

And he touched with his finger tips
Dark boards of elm and alder,
Spruce, and cherry for lathes
That turned all days to spring.

My father's hands were tender
Upon my tender head,
But they were massive on massive
Beam for building a house,

And delicate on the box wood
Leaning against the wall
As though placed there in a corner
For a moment and then forgotten,

And expert as they decoded
Archives unlocked by the axe—
The pretty medullary rays
Once jammed with a traffic of food

To a watched and desired tree
That he marked and felled in the winter,
The tracks of tractors smashing
The ground where violets grew,

Then bound in chains and dragged
To the slaughtering circular saw:
A railway dulcimer
Rang the passing bell

Of my father's loved ones,
Though there was no grief in him
Caressing the slim wood, hearing
A robin's piccolo song.

'DERBYSHIRE BORN, MONMOUTH IS MY HOME'

Derbyshire born, Monmouth is my home,
Monmouth I call Wales, for the voices there
Speak in the songs of Welshmen, and the names
Used every day there—Llantarnum, Pontypool,
Tyn Barlwn, Ebbw Vale—
Are letters from Wales wherever I see them in print.
Caerleon, my youthful home, was a green hill,
A Buddha's belly smiling in a flat field,
Its rondure assimilating for a future age
The marvels of Rome—villas, baths, a bracelet;
And the bridge, too, grey over the yellow Usk,
A thick wide river reminding me of Tiber
In later memory, Tiber unseen,
For Caerleon is all romance and Rome to me—
Brachets and palfreys, the tourney, the hart in the woods,
Imperial roads, the caves of Mithra, fortresses,
And the salt of the ships at Newport and Barry.

Derbyshire born, Monmouth is my home,
Monmouth I call Wales despite cartographers,
My home for a few young years and now,
In spite of Leicestershire that schooled and fought me
And fights me still insisting in my blood.
Yes, Leicester got into my blood and made my bone—
Leicestershire loved me, its stubborn son
Who hated the no man's land, the elbower-out

Of northern and southern culture, possessing none,
I declared in my youthful arrogance:
I saw the cinder paths of mining villages—
Ibstock, Moira, Ellistown—
The chip shop and the corner shop that sold
Racing tips and shameful novelettes;
I saw the dirty pub that loved the colliery
Like its fat and dirtier purse;
And I saw the migrations of miners moving
Across the coalfields from shift to shift
In the red Midland buses they called Red Emmas,
Men's faces black, with rubber-dinghy lips
And floating eyes like nightmare nigger minstrels—
And as I saw I shuddered and cycled on,
Homeless and sick in the towns my home;
Cycled to Charnwood for its hobo roads,
Pre-Cambrian rocks and lonely lapwings,
Rock rose and oak and prairies of fern—
Cycled in solitude to meet a monk
Who stared from a long way off and did not speak.
Charnwood to me was a shape of fear:
Square Teutons of granite, blue jowls
Of bullying slate: I shuddered and ran
To the railway wagons with their owners' names
Painted along their sides like Yankee athletes',
And I was homeless again in Leicestershire.

But Leicester is in my eyes and mind: the Trappist
Tall in the mist, the crags like fangs,

The ruined abbeys, the smell of coal
Have mined in me like secret workings.   Monmouth
I choose, but Leicestershire has chosen,
And lucky I am, reluctant, having a home
To-day when the world is homeless.

‘TO LONDON THE TRAIN GALLOPS, ITS SHRILL STEEL HOOVES’

To London the train gallops, its shrill steel hooves
Pounding the highway in neurotic hurry,
Anxious, it seems, to leave behind the north
With its dialect of hovels and textile mills,
Its cap and muffler fashions, and the soot
Subduing fields gripped in the fists of towns;
And I, in the third-class carriage, pleasantly resign
The flat, stale, and profitable plain
Of the English midlands, where double entry
Is the motto framed on the wall, but where the entry
Is into a cul-de-sac of acclaimed habit,
And double is the P.T. Instructor’s stick
For getting a move on with the getting of cash.
Yes, glad to leave it, the mass-produced
Ambitions, each end of life a dream
Of semi-detachment in a new road
Where the neighbours walk at evening, assessing
Promotion by curtains and caste by the garage
And squabbling for culture as a social asset.

I look forward to London, the huge untidy
Frightening and friendly Johnsonian city—
Chelsea’s conventional unconventionality,
Bloomsbury’s Georgian houses worm-eaten by lodgings,
Charlotte Street pubs where the poets drink their food,

Wide-streeted Kensington, hushed Belgravia, Soho's
Kerbside merchants of invisible merchandise—
London the rich and shabby democrat.
But is this London real, or a town of fancy,
A young romantic's wish? The train goes through
A slum of sidings and locomotive sheds,
Past laundry in backyards and chimney-pots like stumps
In a slattern's mouth—and the commonplace entrance
Gives me a premonition that London, too, may wear
A face familiar as Walsall and the north.

My callow faith in movement ends: perhaps
I am the place and not the places me?

THE DARK CITY

The lighted city is dark, but somewhere a bus
Glows and flares up in a hearth of coal-black space
And with its headlights singles out a face
Lost in a night of enormous loneliness.

Lost in the night of enormous loneliness
Which is his life, man looks for signs of light:
They are the small camp fires which put to flight
The beasts that prowl towards his helplessness.

The beasts that prowl towards our helplessness
Are brave in darkness, but in light they run
To deep subconscious caves in the mind of man
For whom a light is a home in homelessness.

QUARTER SESSIONS: COSH BOY

They can't say what they think, these people of the slums—
Indeed, can't think. The body is a roulette wheel
And the thought is a highly coloured ball that whirls
In a search for release from searching, but never finds
The hole of a word through which to pass into speech:
Returning home the door was locked, love
Had gone into the streets and love was saying to the boy—
Go into the streets and you may find me there.
But the love he wanted wasn't in the streets, so the streets
Took him in and gave him a home and he was happy
Except when remembering the door that was locked. Then
Hatred sought a sentence and faster and faster
Pursued itself in its haste and faster and faster
Raced to escape its pursuer until escape
Came in a gush of lucid rhetoric
Bloody exciting—a work of self-expression
In the boldest romantic idiom of our time.

QUARTER SESSIONS: INCORRIGIBLE ROGUE

From my pew in the jury box, where I sit
With a Bible on a shelf before me giving strength
To my enfeebled self-righteousness I look
At a man in his sin defending sin. He ducks
Under the upraised arm of our stare, then feeling
No summary punishment falling lifts his eyes
To our eyes but hides his eyes at once
Dazzled by a glare that is now a headlight
Swinging to run him down with a blow. He ducks
Under the upraised arm of our stare, then feeling
No summary punishment falling lifts his eyes
To our eyes but hides his eyes at once
Dazzled by a glare that is now a headlight
Swinging to run him down with a blow. He ducks
Under the punishment of his past and lifts his eyes
To the future running him down relentlessly.

BOY'S SONG

I walked as a boy by evergreen hedges
And glancingly fingered their leaves as I passed;
Pictures in colour rose fluttering from them
Complete with accurate field notes of song.

I listened delighted to easy lessons
In a high summer school of brilliant birds—
If this were learning I wanted to be
A scholar of evergreen hedges for ever!

STARLINGS IN TRAFALGAR SQUARE

An image up there like an early film
Flickering through a modern projector,
The starlings circle above the spires,
And the flock is a heart beating.

It is not our heart, we who below
Greet them and hear the foreign chatter—
The starlings inhabit a region of ceilings,
While we on the floors of city ravines
Watch them arriving from the sky
With wonder that ledges of office windows,
Machine-made cherubs and cement corbels
Should be grateful to them as mountain rock.

PIGEON IN LONDON

Dove-grey dove in the ash-tree
Plucking at leaves, like a gourmet
With fidgety precision picking the tender shoots,
But like a gourmand gobbling with a gulp
And returning for more with a fanatic's concentration.

You lean so far in love with succulence
You will lose your balance and on your perch
Swing like a broken pivot, your permit to work
In this foreign country withdrawn. But you do not fall.
Your papers are in order. You proclaim your citizenship
In these town gardens as with wings in air,
Dove-grey dove they call the wood-pigeon.

SNOW AT BOIS D'ARCY

Someone opened the shutters
And a dazzle of sea-gulls beat up the room,
Hammering my head beneath the sheets
And lashing the lids of my eyes
With the sternness of their brightness.
At first I closed my ears
Against the clarion of their colour
That pierced my no with the prod of yes—
But the tines of light sank deep
And hurt me alive: there was so much violence
Battering the room, so much anger
Agonizing my eyes that I awoke
To protect myself from whiteness.

ST MARY'S, BOLTONS

The spire pierces the charming
Appearance of Kensington like a thorn;
Cushioned on poplar and sycamore
This splinter of a crown

In the Royal Borough gathers
Up the tender afternoon light
And hurls it at the parish
Brutally bright.

Whiteness is the impression, in spite of the many
Many-coloured ping-pong balls that bubble
Above the bridge like an early Piper or Nicholson
Abstract; whiteness is the impression, whiteness
Of bath-tiles, dairies, hospitals, whiteness
Of hygiene in the mind cleaned of irrelevance;
Also whiteness of sunlight glittering on limestone
Alps, of sea-gulls flecking a concrete
Esplanade, waved handkerchiefs, whiteness
Of hygiene in the emotions, a tonic pleasure.

And whiteness in this double aspect
Of purgation and creation is the colour of buildings
Likely to be blown flat by blast and deliberately
Jauntily impermanent; whiteness is the colour
Of this whirling playpen where windmills and balloons
And amusing ornaments turn out to be radar aerials
And water wittily fails to cancel fire;
And whiteness is the colour of the Dome: with its queue
Coiled round like string it may be a top or science,
But is certainly science happily spinning a yarn—
For in this exhibition of national talents
The line-shooting we see is the throw-away line
Of a civilization underplaying its doubt;
It is a whiteness that may be black, a blackness
Very white indeed in our plastic arts
And architecture of airfields: a purgation of fear,
Creation of disbelief in doom's day.

THE CORNER SHOP

I remember it away from London
In the English midlands of mines and pottery kilns
And vowels as flat as the earth
Around Nuneaton. But Leicestershire,
Warwickshire, or Derby—what does it matter?
All corner shops are alike and all unlike
All other shops: only they can nourish
The growing boy—it may be sherbet
Suckers and dabs, straps of liquorice,
Ice cream cornets or aniseed,
Or it may be an envelope sealed
Off from the innocent eye and beginning
The end of innocence, or it may be
Sweet cigarettes to swank with and swallow,
Or marbles and tops mixed up
In a jumble sale where comic
Postcards scorch the face that goes too near
And string is chewing gum and chewing gum
Elastic and elastic is the corner
Departmental store and tobacconist,
Bookseller, grocer, universal provider
Of food for thought to the boy
Who visits it daily and wonders
What is around the corner.

'AS A BOY WITH A RICHNESS OF NEEDS I WANDERED'

As a boy with a richness of needs I wandered
In car parks and streets, epicure of Lagondas,
Minervas, Invictas, and Hispano Suizas;
And I sampled as roughage and amusing sauce
Little Rovers and Rileys, and the occasional funny
Trojan with chain drive, and the Morris Cowleys
With their modest bonnets, sedate Fiat
Of the nineteen-twenties, and the Alvis, middle-brow
Between the raffish sports car and the family bus.
I was tempted by aircraft, too, sniffing
Over *The Aeroplane* and *Flight*—those kites,
They seem to-day, knocked up in a backyard
By young and oily artists who painted with rivets:
Westland Wapiti, Bristol Bulldog, and the great
De Havilland Hercules, invading the desert
And pulsing within its sleep like a troubling nerve;
And surely, I think, as I remember those feasts,
They were days of excitement and lavish surprise?
Where is the tantalizing richness and hazard
Of assertive styling, of crazy rigs,
Now that a car is unremarkably one of a million,
And an aeroplane is a tubular schedule? I wander
Still in the car parks, but now uneasily,
Thinking that engineering is a sort of evolution—
Out of the fittest come the many merely fit;
And I wonder if I am wrong, or the world, whose aspect
Is nowhere strange, but is nowhere home.

THE MOTH

Enjoying a council house's ration
  Of lawn where a year ago
Wood owls scratched at the darkness, squawking
  For a tasty rat or shrew,

And where in the daytime children came
  To pick wild flowers, to climb
The trees in a New England of freedom
  Not far and far from home,

My head beneath a hawthorn-tree,
  My feet in wild chervil
Excavated away with dock,
  Daisy, and cinquefoil,

I sat in a deck-chair, shut in by a fence
  High, creosoted, brown,
That carved a box of privacy
  Out of the wide and green,

And there I read my books of travel—
  The poems of John of the Cross,
The Cloud of Unknowing, *The Song of the Lord*,
  The Imitation of Christ:

I read of Thoreau, rich by discovering
  So much that he did not want;
Of Borrow happy in affairs of Egypt
  Or tinkering in a tent

On the Great North Road, not so remote
  From the midland town where I
Turned the pages and heard an engine
  And had to glance away

To look at a biplane, very small,
  And flying so far above
Cauliflowers, clothes-lines, and cycle sheds
  That it seemed it did not move.

But soon I saw it certainly moving—
  Quitting the sky and slanting down
As though to fall in the market-place.
  I left my book and ran

Through the baulks of brick, keeping my face
  Turned to the aeroplane
Striding ahead of me, miles to my feet,
  Three villages beyond the town.

Why was I racing past houses and hedges?
  What did I hope to see?
The lapis philosophorum? The Kingdom?
  Buddha's bodhi-tree?

Why did I run so fast through the summer,
  The only caring boy?
Did I hope for a hero? The ideal friend?
  The not impossible she?

For an hour or more I ran, not knowing
  What I was hoping to find
But fearing exactly what it would be—
  A crock of foils in a field:

A D.H. Moth, wingless, dead.
  I turned away from the wreck
And went through the lanes back to the town
  And my council house and book.

MY FORMER SELF

I speak to him and he doesn't answer.
   Does he hear, I wonder?
Why does he look around in the garden
   With so much wonder?

Why should I mind that every moment
   He wants to treasure?
He pulls up butterfly after butterfly
   As he digs for treasure.

He reaches up into the sunlight
   And picks flower after flower
In a broken looking-glass garden
   Where seed runs to flower.

THE CHILDREN

Quietly the children wait
With eyes that shine like knives
Brightening the fading world
Through which I daily walk
My grown uncertain way from death to life.

Untaught and unafraid
They watch with their blades bare,
Blades where appetite glistens
As on visionary tongues
Keen to cut at a world that tastes so new.

Once, a child, I waited
Like children waiting now;
I, too, had surgeon's eyes
That instantaneously
Severed from time all time except to-morrow.

I, too, looked at the parents
Making a home for me;
Using trowel and timber,
But more their heart and brain:
I saw a home that I was born to destroy.

I am the builder now
As once my father built,
Using his trowel and timber
And some of his heart and brain
To build a home unlike his but the same—

And quietly the children wait,
Their eyes shining like knives
Brightening the fading world
Through which I daily walk
My grown uncertain way from life to death.

POEM FOR MY BIRTHDAY

The trees cry in my ear
In this saddened month of January;
Everywhere I look are fields
Tearful as the sky.

The birds are silent, dumb
With mourning cold; the hedges wear
Summer foliage grievously dark
For the funeral of the year.

I tread the tomb and laugh:
I know that where I am standing soon
I shall see the stiff year up and about
And ask: who moved the stone?

SONG FOR THE BIRTHDAY OF A CHILD AGED THREE YEARS AND TEN MONTHS

For Susan Mackie

Clownquick the fountains
Plummet the sky,
Soaring to the full stop
Of infinity—

Washing the pay dirt
Out of space
And into a purse
Of milksoft lace—

As full as the future
With money to spend:
Girl,
Each day is your birthday—

May it never end

TALKING TO GIRLS

By a coincidence it was the spring
When I talked to the girls in the school near trees
And an acre of flowers. The house that held us
Clung to the sloping lawn like a red berry
In a moment rolling away, and I inside it
Was dazed as I lectured about books to the girls
Who sat with clock-like faces motionless
But were inwardly irresistibly driven by spring.
I talked with propriety, but I was dizzy
With the bursting energy of this berry
That wanted to tear itself up and away
In the pull of the season that was pulling me.

MEDITATION ON THE WORD GIRDLE

'In ancient times, the wearing of a girdle, which was supposed to divide the pure upper part of the body from the lower part, was considered the fulfilment of a religious command.'—*Chambers's Encyclopaedia*.

Through sash or girdle was slung
Greek chiton; from belt or girdle hung
Medieval sword or inkhorn; it is poetry
(In Shakespeare powerful fantasy,
Simple and charming in Waller, Tennyson);
And girdles are the rings that run
Like an elastic second skin
Guarding the frontier of sin,
Distinguishing the pure above
From the lower carnal love,
Though (as I hold no brief
For asceticism) it is my belief
Such girdles do not separate
The impure from the pure estate,
But represent the physical
Marriage with the spiritual;
In their embrace they span
Man and woman, woman and man,
All opposites for whom opposition
Is fulfilled in union,
All opposites that must give
Life that opposites might live.

GOTHAM HILL, NOTTINGHAMSHIRE

The road was an excellent partner. We climbed
Agreeably together on the slow ascent until
We reached the summit—and then I found myself
On the hilltop alone: the road had taken a leap
On to its love below and looking far down
I saw they had met and become one flesh.

‘THE RHONDDA HILLS ARE TALL AND LEAN’

The Rhondda hills are tall and lean
Like greyhounds stripped-down for speed,
But the townships running close at their feet
Are going all out to take the lead.

The long-legged hills and the puffing towns
Are neck to neck in this hard race:
The towns lack style but are full of tricks
And the hills are tough in spite of their grace.

‘IN THE TRAIN JUST OUTSIDE CARDIFF’

In the train just outside Cardiff
We were jammed together, the lot of us,
Helping ourselves to each other and instruments
To us—trombones, clarinets, gourmandizing euphoniums.

We were jolly, on our way to a blow-out
At the Eisteddfod—miners, typists, men from the hills
And the tin-plate workers from the valley towns,
Holiday spirits going to our heads.

A bass rolled out a song that was like a barrel,
A tenor answered in wine, white and dry:
By the time the train pulled up at the musical station
We were all quite drunk and proud of our beautiful prizes.

SALZBURG

I saw it in summer and that is the season
Of Salzburg for ever: the sky and the sun
Are the fellows of blue and gold frescoes warming
The cupboard-dark churches like burning arrows
Forcing barred windows at noon; and domes
Of copper and green are bunches of fruit
Well on the way to ripeness. In replete
Episcopal squares the traveller shelters
From heat in the rain of fountains falling
Into marble basins to glockenspiel music:
For listening, looking, and loving are the only
Pursuits of this city—a civilization
Here rests perpetually at the peak
Where the arts are a conversation enjoyed
By men in a bivouac pitched between
An ascetic ascent and a bawdy decline.

WILDER KAISER

Seeds trickle into shoes, the air is sprayed
With the music of grasshoppers greener than grass
On which sun spreads itself like butter, turning
Pasture into a Breughelian banquet of flowers.

Matured to a delicate cream by who knows how
Much seasoning the Wilder Kaiser is heaped
On a plateau near the sky, a food so regal
That only eagles can get their claws on it.

BAHNHOFSTRASSE

Night slides down the mountain side
In an avalanche unheard, the dust
Rolling into the streets of Zürich
As mist moth-soft towards the lights:
It wraps up brooches of glass in gauzes,
Clocks are diamond pendants worn
By a wealth of space, women are flattering
Soft focus portraits, the flashing
Foyers of cafés are enormous carnivals
Of orchids and roses, the air is furry
Lined against snow and solitude.

JOYCE IN ZÜRICH

Grey city with the gay life
Lived in radio programmes
Of peasants yodelling; grey city
Of houses cast in cement, where blue
Trams pick their routes as neatly
As fishes through a confluence
Of streams; grey city
Effacing and practical that dismayed
Rilke, but gave James Joyce a home for years.
Ask the people of Zürich
About James Joyce and they do not know,
Do not remember the poor-eyed Irishman
Who lived among them listening: for his
Was another capital than theirs, his
Was never a neutral country.
The streets he walked were the wide
Zürich streets flanked by Georgian cafés;
There was a Hauptstrasse called Grafton
Or O'Connell Street; and there was water,
The waters of, the Liffeying waters of
Another capital than this; and there was talk,
But not his own, for his own was not
In Dublin, nor in Zürich;
Nor in London, Trieste, or Paris.
Joyce is not remembered in Zürich because
His own was what he was, wherever he was—
A country in all countries and like none,

Recalling the look of familiar places
But unfamiliar in the moment of recognition.
That country demanded a language
Unique, like its geography, and Joyce
Spoke this and more and more only this
In the streets grey and by the lake green-grey
Of the unnoticed unnoticing city he called home.

WRITING IS NOT WRITING

Writing is not writing, it is not
With ink or pencil day after day
Cancelling pages like leaves of a calendar,
Words an acid eating a way through time.
This is praiseworthy; it is not pleasure;
It is profit, turnover, very visible export—
Who intrudes hurries away, recognizing work.
But writing is not work.   The writer
Writing is an idler—the observer thinks—sitting
On top of a bus staring through the window
Of a train, reading another writer's writing,
Lunching all afternoon, or lonely in the park
Watching the water and the water birds—
This is not working, but a waste of writing:
For writing is not writing, it is growing
Accustomed to oneself, it is learning
To live with the stranger who lives with strangers
And who can only be known by patiently not trying
Too much: for growth is slow and to the observer
Is not growing, as writing is not writing.

'DESPAIR IS A SHARER OF MY HOUSE'

Despair is a sharer of my house:
I hear a knock
And when I open the door
No one is there: only
Despair. I hear
A creak on the stair,
Feel the air move
Over my face,
See the page darken and feel the presence
Behind my chair, but when I turn
No one is there: only
Despair sits at my desk,
Shakes the curtains, pads on the carpet,
Crosses the corridor,
Goes and comes on the stair—
With such affectionate care
For me that I am sure
No one is there
Sharing my house when I am alone:
Not even despair.

'THE SILKEN ROADS OF DECEIT'

The silken roads of deceit
    Lead easily
    To brilliant inns
Blazing in night a trail
Of invitations to hearths
Where one can hide from the cold,
Cold most bitter in the night
    When man withdraws
From sharing the complete pain
    Of his fellow man.

The silken roads of deceit
    Too easily
    Are travelled by those
Locked in space alone
Where man is unable to escape
From man because they are bound
In a love mistaken for hate.
    The silken roads
Lead gratefully to peace
    As ruinous as war.

THE SUICIDE

I reject the world for I know that the world
   Has rejected me.   Now
I can be arrogant who have envied arrogance
   All through life like love.

At last I have the integrity of those
   Who do not wish for favours:
In this moment of death I am living
   For the first time without fear

Because for the first time without hope.
   I do not long for a no
To soothe like a yes: that was a need
   It is my gain to lack.

JESUS AND CHRIST

Glad the priests and scribes beholding
  That man from Nazareth,
The seditious teacher, caught on the Cross
  And visibly dumb in death.

But the visible was illusion. A man
  Whose name was Jesus died,
But with his mortal breath he spoke
  Christ, the immortal Word.

'THE SEA IS A ROCK'

i

The sea is a rock
The rock is a lake
The lake is a cloud
The cloud is a sea

The sea and the rock and the lake and the cloud
Are one

But the bird is a hunter
Elsewhere

The bird opposes

And I
Watching the bird?

ii

I oppose
As man opposes
Opposing himself

Brass
Clangs in the shivering
Equatorial air

Brass
Clangs in the glass bells
Of the earth's ice caps
Brass
Clangs and the lion quietens
Brass
Clangs and the reindeer stops
Brass
Clangs from the challenging cave

The music of the world is broken

iii

The crowns of the sea
Are raised on a wave of pride
And fall
In a misery of mist
And lost
Where the fish is safe

The hearths of our houses
Cheer and char

How can justice end
In a split second? we cry
Foreknowing the bomb

iv

Words of the sea
Bird: startle and lift
Me on your wings

Fountain me
Bird
In your wings and words

I would be borne
As a feather of song
On the breath of choirs

Borne aloft
Born anew

v

The guts of the sea
Plectrumed by rocks
Sing
A nativity hymn

The man of stone
And the woman of water
Make
A child of harmony

Silenced

By the clang man makes beating the world